THE COURAGE OF IGNORANCE

THE COURAGE OF IGNORANCE

By

WILLIAM LYON PHELPS

William Lyon Phelps

William Lyon Phelps was born on 2nd January 1865, in New Haven, Conneticut, United States.

Phelps earned a B.A. in 1887, writing his thesis on the Idealism of George Berkeley. He then gained an M.A. in 1891 from Yale and his PhD from Harvard in the same year. During his time a Yale, he offered a course in modern novels which brought the university considerable attention both nationally and internationally. This was quite controversial at the time and Phelps was pressured to give up the course, but eventually, due to popular demand, reinstated it outside the official curriculum.

In 1892, Phelps married Annabel Hubbard, sister of childhood friend Frank Hubbard, and the couple moved to the family estate overlooking Lake Huron. Phelps christened it "The House of the Seven Gables", after the Nathanial Hawthorne story of the same name.

He became a very popular figure at Yale but also as an

inspirational orator. He went on lecture tours that drew large audiences, speaking on the virtues of modern literature. He also preached regularly at the Huron City Methodist Episcopal Church and attracted such large crowds that the church was remodelled twice in five years to accommodate them.

Phelps published many essays on modern and European literature, including titles such as *Essays on Modern Novelists* (1910), *Some Makers of American Literature* (1923), and *As I Like it* (1923).

After his retirement from Yale in 1933, after 41 years of service, Phelps continued his public speaking, preaching, and writing a newspaper column. He also sat on book selection committees and acted as a judge for the Pulitzer Prize for literature.

His wife, Annabel, died from a stroke in 1939 and Phelps died four years later, in 1943.

"Greet the unseen with a cheer!"
—*Browning.*

THE COURAGE OF IGNORANCE

THE COURAGE OF IGNORANCE

Υ

COURAGE is not the greatest of the virtues, because so many abominable persons have it; and cowardice is not the blackest sin, though a display of cowardice brings general contempt. Cruelty, ingratitude, treachery, are all worse faults than cowardice; yet many men who are cruel, ungrateful and treacherous, live in the sunshine of popular favour.

THE COURAGE

Although courage is not the greatest of the virtues, it may be regarded as the basis of many virtues. J. M. Barrie did well in quoting Doctor Johnson, who said "Unless a man has that virtue, he has no security for preserving any other." But Doctor Johnson made reservations:

> We talked of a certain clergyman of extraordinary character, who by exerting his talents in writing on temporary topics, and displaying uncommon intrepidity, had raised himself to affluence. I maintained that we ought not to be indignant at his success; for merit of every sort was entitled to reward. Johnson: "Sir, I will not allow this man to have merit. No, sir; what he has is rather the contrary; I will, indeed, allow him courage, and on this account we so far give him credit. We have more respect for a man who robs boldly on the highway, than for a fellow who jumps out of a ditch, and knocks you down behind your back. Courage is a quality so neces-

OF IGNORANCE

sary for maintaining virtue, that it is always respected, even when it is associated with vice."

Courage is necessary not only in adventurous and hazardous enterprises, but in average daily living. Women perhaps have more courage than men, because they need it more. It takes courage just to be a woman.

> Tell me, are men unhappy, in some kind
> Of mere unhappiness at being men,
> As women suffer, being womanish?

Seven times in the Old Testament it says, "Be of good courage." There is a fine text in the twenty-seventh Psalm: "Wait on the Lord: be of good courage, and he shall strengthen thine heart: wait, I say, on the Lord." Reverence and energy, the co-operation of man with God, is not a bad com-

THE COURAGE

bination. Oliver Cromwell expressed it concretely when he told his soldiers to trust in God, and to keep their powder dry.

Of all the varieties of endowment, the intellectual capital that we receive at birth, perhaps the most extraordinary, the most mysterious, and the most weighty in determining the individual's happiness or misery, is the Power of Choice. Surely most of us are quite unfitted for such a tremendous responsibility. It is as if we gathered in a room a thousand children three years old, gave to each one a sharp knife, and then left them without supervision. Some would kill others, some would kill themselves, and only a very few would turn so dangerous an implement into constructive work. Thus men may make their lives interesting to themselves, and valuable to others, or they may be mere architects of disaster. But

OF IGNORANCE

character can be developed only through the power of choice. Even God cannot get our vote unless we give it.

With only cloudy intelligence, with animal impulses stronger than foresight or wisdom, with no power to read the future, with ignorance not only of others but of ourselves, it is surprising that so many people make even a moderate success of life. To go forward requires both wisdom and courage.

In the old days, when theological discussions were more common than they are now, devout persons felt much difficulty in attempting to reconcile the power of choice with the foreknowledge of God. In my boyhood I frequently heard discussions concerning predestination and free will. Possibly the best solution of that problem was furnished by a coloured preacher in the

THE COURAGE

South: "God predestines every man to be saved. The Devil predestines every man to be damned. Man has the casting vote."

Out of this dilemma Browning, in characteristic fashion, maintained that the individual soul found the possibility of development. For the only Holy War, with no ending and no armistice, is the civil war in every human heart.

> No, when the fight begins within himself,
> A man's worth something. God stoops o'er his head,
> Satan looks up between his feet—both tug—
> He's left himself, i' the middle: the soul wakes
> And grows. Prolong that battle through his life!

I say there can be (with only one exception) no courage—either physical or moral—without ignorance. The courage of ig-

OF IGNORANCE

norance is true courage. If a man *knew* on entering a fist fight or a duel with swords that he would eventually win, his audacities would rise not from courage, but from special and exclusive information. If we *knew* in the much more important contest of daily living, that virtue would certainly be rewarded, it would require not courage, but caution, to run straight. Courage is where one does his best in uncertainty as to the outcome.

This is why the tangible rewards of virtue, as they were once set forth in the old-fashioned Sunday School story, and are now set forth in the new-fashioned motion pictures, arouse the laughter of incredulity. We know very well that life is not so easy as all that.

If courage were based on knowledge rather than on ignorance, then Mark

THE COURAGE

Twain's jest would be more generally applicable: "I have often admired the calm confidence of a Christian—with four aces."

I mentioned an exception. The exception is where there is knowledge and yet courage. This knowledge is the knowledge of defeat rather than of victory. Even here there is a fine distinction between this noble courage and the mere blind courage of despair, which I shall discuss later. Suppose a young man enters a football game with the usual mental attitude; he hopes to win, he knows he may lose, but he means to do his best. The game proceeds and is almost over; there are only five minutes left to play; his opponents have forty points and his side nothing. Obviously he is as certainly beaten as if the final whistle had blown. Has he any choice left? Of course he has. He can now lose like a

OF IGNORANCE

craven or like a gentleman. He can quit or he can still fight.

> I am near the end; but still not at the end;
> All to the very end is trial in life:
> At this stage is the trial of my soul
> Danger to face, or danger to refuse? . . .
> Still, I stand here, not off the stage though close
> On the exit: and my last act, as my first I owe the scene.

One of the most stirring and poignant passages in literature is where Hector takes farewell of his wife and child before going forth into battle. His wife Andromache besought him not to venture out for fear of death.

> Then great Hector of the glancing helm answered her: "Surely I take thought for all these things, my wife; but I have very sore shame of the Tro-

THE COURAGE

jans and Trojan dames with trailing robes, if like a coward I shrink away from battle. Moreover mine own soul forbiddeth me, seeing I have learnt ever to be valiant and fight in the forefront of the Trojans, winning my father's great glory and mine own. Yea of a surety I know this in heart and soul; the day shall come for holy Ilios to be laid low, and Priam and the folk of Priam of the good ashen spear."

The gallant Cyrano de Bergerac exclaimed that the best of all fighting was when defeat was certain. I suppose he meant it was the severest test of manhood.

Emily Brontë, cursed with ill health and with no hope of happiness, wrote:

> But when the days of golden dreams had perished,
> And even Despair was powerless to destroy,
> Then did I learn how existence could be cherished,

OF IGNORANCE

> Strengthened and fed, without the aid of joy.

Many men and women have been crushed by despair; but some brave souls have learned not only to endure but to *advance,* even after their last hope of happiness has vanished, even after they "have nothing to look forward to." I suppose we all know some men and women, who, after appalling calamities, are neither wearily supine nor grimly defiant; but somehow manage to go ahead and do their daily work minus every trace of happiness. The faces of children are expectant; they look as if they were about to receive something delightful; but there are men and women who positively *know* that tomorrow and the next week will be not one bit better than today; and yet they go forward. They deserve our homage.

THE COURAGE

All these cases furnish the one exception to the general rule; here is where courage exists with knowledge, instead of arising from ignorance. Fortunately, only comparatively few persons are forced to meet this supreme test.

Nothing arouses more instant enthusiasm than a display of physical courage; it makes one want to shout and cheer. We do well to salute; and yet physical courage in the mass, group-courage, the courage of soldiers in desperate battles, sublime as it is, is very common. It is indeed the regular and expected thing. It has always been true of disciplined soldiers, in ancient and modern times. No period of history, no nation, no race, has any monopoly of this splendid virtue. A black man will fight in a group just as well as a white, a yellow man as well as a brown, a red man as well

OF IGNORANCE

as a black. The "cause" makes no difference whatever. Soldiers will fight just as well for a bad cause as for a good one. And even hired soldiers, soldiers of fortune who sell their strength for pay, even as a professional man sells his brains, will fight as well as volunteers. A. E. Housman wrote a poem on the Mercenaries, who stood firm in battle and saved civilisation after the volunteers and even God had deserted the cause.

Nor does the hope of reward make any difference. Kipling's poem on Fuzzy-Wuzzy shows that although Fuzzy-Wuzzy had no distinguished service medal or Victoria Cross or honourable mention or promotion to look forward to, he "broke a British square."

It is easy enough to understand how men, after months of training and disci-

THE COURAGE

pline, could march (with appropriate music) into danger; but what makes them stay there? In a certain battle, where the troops were besieging a walled town, a breach was made in the wall, and the order was given to advance. It was a certainty that the first fifty or sixty men who reached the hole in the wall would be blown to pieces. Well, did they hesitate? Did they say, "After you, Gaston?" Did any of them pretend to be lame and let the others outstrip them in the race to the horrible goal? No! they ran for that wall with more eagerness than men run for a prize; and the first fifty or sixty were annihilated.

What makes men in all times and of all nations behave in this sublime fashion? The universal courage of soldiers is a mystery. I have asked many men who have fought in bloody battles for an explana-

OF IGNORANCE

tion, and I have never received an answer that was satisfactory. One soldier told me there were in every general engagement more cowards, deserters, and sneaks than was known by the folks at home; but even so, they constitute only a very small minority. I suppose the feeling that drives men forward into danger is a compound of bravery, fear, shame, discipline, rage, desire to win, crowd-spirit, and other more obscure emotional mixtures. Sublime as it is, it happens to be so universal, that we cannot determine whether or not a man has courage simply because he did his duty in the ranks.

Courage is an emotion that transcends common sense. If it were true that men regard death as the greatest of misfortunes, it would be easier than it is now to make predictions as to what the average man

THE COURAGE

would do in emergencies. But the sublime fact is that not only an exceptional hero, but millions of men will fling away their lives for more than a few reasons.

It is interesting to observe that the average man is condemned and disgraced in war for the very thing for which people often praise him in times of peace. We are all familiar with the so-called hard-headed person whose sole concern is his own welfare. In ordinary days he ridicules self-sacrifice, philanthropies, and all the actions born of what he regards as unintelligent enthusiasms; his policy is crudely but clearly expressed in such phrases as "I'm going this way only once, and I intend to make the most of it," "I shall be a long time dead," "It's all the same a hundred years from now," "You mind your business and I'll mind mine," etc., etc. Frankly, al-

OF IGNORANCE

though I have for this so-called canny person no feeling except contempt, there are many who express admiration. "He drives a hard bargain, but he's nobody's fool," "His head's screwed on tight," etc. Yet when this interesting self-centred gentleman behaves in that same way in battle, then everyone despises him as a coward. The reason is obvious; but the man is consistent, true to form. "What did you run for?" "Why, you idiot, you don't understand. They were shooting at us! Do you suppose I intend to get hit?" "But it's dishonourable!" "Well, who is honourable?"

> Honour pricks me on. Yea, but how if honour prick me off when I come on? how then? Can honour set to a leg? No. Or an arm? No. Or take away the grief of a wound? No. Honour hath no skill in surgery then? No. What is honour? a word. What is that word, honour? Air.

THE COURAGE

A trim reckoning! Who hath it? he that died o' Wednesday. Doth he feel it? No. Doth he hear it? No. It is insensible then? Yea, to the dead.

Courage is greater than common sense and reason, for there is no *rational* answer to the above soliloquy.

But as personal courage is higher than common sense, so is it deeper. In that remarkable lecture, *The Name and Nature of Poetry,* delivered at Cambridge in 1933 by the great poet A. E. Housman, he made the following comment:

> "Whosoever will save his life shall lose it and whosoever will lose his life shall find it." That is the most important truth which has ever been uttered, and the greatest discovery ever made in the moral world.

At about the same time this lecture was

OF IGNORANCE

delivered, the Irish poet, Padraic Colum, had an article in *The Commonweal* called "To be Only Wise is not Wisdom," beginning:

> Once, when I was walking down a street in Dublin with him, John Butler Yeats said to me, "Our liking for people is in inverse ratio to their sense of self-preservation," and this saying explained to me why certain very admirable people are often not warmly liked by us—their sense of self-preservation obscurely realized by us diminishes the liking that we might expect to have for them. And then I thought that it needs a dramatic confrontation to show us that no matter how admirable certain people of importance may be, they have not a character that we can truly venerate and love, since they lack the quality which overbalances their sense of self-preservation.

This acute analysis may help to explain our immense admiration for those whose

THE COURAGE

outstanding quality is courage. Remember that the Gospel was hidden from the prudent. Indeed, prudence is so poor a virtue that it is hardly a virtue at all. President Eliot of Harvard once said to me, "Prudence is not an especially desirable quality in a college professor."

We have seen that group-courage, however thrilling, is nevertheless common; thus the only way to discover whether an individual is brave, is to isolate him from the crowd, and see how he behaves when alone in danger. Bacon said, "Men fear death as children fear to go in the dark." But the fear of going in the dark is by no means confined to children. Grown men and women fear to go in the dark. There is hardly a man or woman who would like to enter without any light at two o'clock

OF IGNORANCE

in the morning an unoccupied house, and climb the stairs and go from room to room. No matter how stoutly one might attempt to reassure oneself by forced soliloquies to the effect that there was no danger, if one has any imagination, one has also fear. But the curious thing is, that if a man entered a lonely house in the night, accompanied by a little child, the man would not be afraid. If trouble should come, the child would be a liability rather than an asset; but the mere living company of another human being helps to take away fear.

Thus, to discover the higher qualities of physical courage, we must study the behaviour of a man either alone or friendless. History furnishes some magnificent illustrations.

I suppose there never lived a man of more

THE COURAGE

desperate, reckless courage than the Englishman Robert Clive (1725-1774). It is perhaps fortunate for the United States of America that he did not live a few years longer and lead an English army against our troops. The actual story of Clive's life is so filled with improbabilities, where the "thing that couldn't" occurred over and over again, that if it were a novel instead of fact, readers would regard it as impossibly romantic. Indeed, it seems to me strange that in our age when biographical writing is such a temptation to seekers for sensation, more biographies of this king of adventurers have not appeared. I know of only one. Clive is still a magic name in India; an Englishman who had just returned from many years of residence there, told me the surest name to stir an instant response was that of Lord Clive.

OF IGNORANCE

Even as a boy, Clive had in him to a superlative degree an unquenchable thirst for excitement and adventure. Of course all normal boys and girls have something of this, girls I think even more commonly and more fiercely than boys. Some day economists, philosophers, teachers, preachers will learn what ought to be obvious; the very simple truth that most human beings prefer excitement to comfort. Many grave social philosophers imagine that if every person had enough money to remove anxiety for the immediate future, they would all be satisfied. But the history of human nature shows plainly that people prefer dangerous adventures to stagnant security. It is instructive to reread the Gospels solely from that point of view, and observe just what advantages Our Lord promised to those who were willing to fol-

THE COURAGE

low Him; and then compare these promises with those of the average politician seeking election. One who did not know human nature would imagine that after listening to the programme of Jesus, no one would have had anything more to do with Him. On the contrary, enormous crowds followed Him whithersoever He went.

Why is it that if a war should break out tomorrow, millions of young men and women would eagerly leave all their luxuries and comforts and enlist? Their only fear would be that they might not arrive in time to take an active part. No one will ever understand the spirit of youth until he understands this.

Now what is universal in youth was in Clive heightened almost to the pitch of madness. As the hart panteth for the

OF IGNORANCE

waterbrooks, so panted he for excitement and adventure. And no youth then living had apparently less chance of gratifying this passion. He was a clerk totting up accounts day after day on a miserable salary. So utterly disgusted was he with this way of existence and with the bleak prospect, that one day he took from his desk a loaded pistol, placed the muzzle against his face and pulled the trigger. The pistol failed to explode. Now whether suicide be an act of cowardice or courage, it is generally true that when a wretched man finally nerves himself up to shoot himself, and the weapon fails to go off, he calls it a day.

More time passed in the same dreary round of intolerable dullness. And again with another loaded pistol Clive pulled the trigger, and again with no result. A friend of his came into the room and Clive asked him to take this same weapon, go to the open window, aim it into the air, and pull the trigger. People always did what Clive asked them to do. So, although considerably puzzled, his friend did his bidding, and behold, there was a tremendous report. Clive was a born gambler; he said to himself that he must be reserved for something great.

He was; by a series of events that would be incredible if they were not a matter of record, he became a General in the British Army, the Conqueror of India, the Governor General of India, a multimillionaire, a peer of the realm—and then, with his work done, and still not fifty years old, he committed suicide.

It was Clive who gave India to England, and although it is a hot handful, England

OF IGNORANCE

has it still, and I hope she will never give it up.

Now of all the numerous desperate adventures where Clive showed unflinching courage, perhaps the greatest was while he was still a clerk and was playing cards with the military officers. Although these gentry despised civilians, they permitted Clive to play with them, because he had what was later to be known as a "poker face." He never betrayed any emotion during or after a game of cards; although he secretly must have wondered why he lost so often. One evening, when he was the only civilian in a roomful of officers, and was himself playing with a Captain, he suddenly caught the Captain cheating. It is probable that the officer felt safe even if detected, because he did not think that Clive would dare speak, which shows that he was insufficiently acquainted with his quiet opponent. Instantly Clive exclaimed "You cheated!" The Captain pretended not to understand; but Clive left him in no doubt. Then the Captain tried to bluff it out by saying contemptuously that he supposed a clerk did not understand the consequences of insulting a gentleman. Clive replied that the sooner they settled the matter the better. Accordingly seconds were appointed, a clear space was made in the room, each was furnished with a loaded pistol, and told that at the word they could fire. Clive fired at the very moment and missed. Then under the rules of the duel at that time, the Captain had a free shot in cold blood at Clive. (This is the way Andrew Jackson murdered his opponent.)

The Captain pointed the deadly weapon at Clive and wishing to torture him before

OF IGNORANCE

killing him, enquired "Did I cheat?" and Clive replied,

"*Go to hell!*"

I wonder if all of my readers realise what courage it took to face a man with a loaded pistol, and give him that invitation. I do. When I was young, I was held up in the West one night by a man who held a loaded revolver six inches in front of my nose. I could see the raised hammer, the lead in the chambers, and the man's finger on the trigger. I did not tell him to go anywhere; I gave him my watch. Afraid? I was horribly afraid, so afraid that I was very careful not to irritate him in any way or to make any movement. I can therefore appreciate the desperate reckless courage of Clive.

So far as I can discover, Clive was one of those exceedingly rare individuals, per-

THE COURAGE

haps one in a million, who did not know the sensation of physical fear. Most persons I think are instinctively cowards, even as most persons are instinctively selfish; which makes the sight of so many brave men and so many unselfish men all the more inspiring.

I had always supposed that Marshal Ney was without physical fear, until I heard a story about him at the battle of Waterloo. It will be remembered that Napoleon—a good judge of courage—called Ney the bravest of the brave, and indeed his behaviour during the long retreat from Moscow is a revelation of the possible grandeur of human nature. But it seems that on the morning at Waterloo, as he was climbing into the saddle, a sudden horrible fear took possession of him. *Ney was afraid.*

OF IGNORANCE

Do his utmost, he could not control the shaking of his knees. Raging because of this trembling, he looked at his knees and said, "Shake away, knees! You would shake worse than that, if you knew where I was going to take you!"

My admiration for Ney became almost adoration when I heard that story.

For perhaps that is the highest form of courage, the conquest of the body by the mind. The population of the earth may be divided into two classes: those whose bodies control their minds, and those whose minds control their bodies. Ney's body did not want to go into battle; but up in the conning-tower of the body is the brain, and the brain said to the knees, "I am deciding this matter, not you. You are afraid? Well, I will give you something to be afraid of,

THE COURAGE

in order that you may find out who is in command." That day he had five horses shot under him.

The body expresses a desire for something, and the mind says, "This is not good for you!" But the body insists and the mind yields. It may be so simple a matter as getting up in the morning. The alarm clock rings and the mind says, "Get up!" but the body says, "Just another ten minutes!" and the mind yields, not realising that right there future failure in a more important matter has been decided. Perhaps a man is better off when he knows in advance his own weakness, as knowledge of oneself is so rare. Years ago there was a Yale student who knew that if he did not rise at half-past seven the next morning and go to chapel, he might be suspended from college. He therefore wrote out a huge plac-

OF IGNORANCE

ard and placed it on the outside of his door, for the benefit of the janitor.

> **JANITOR**
> WAKE ME AT 7.30 IN THE MORNING
> MAKE NO MISTAKE
> NO MATTER WHAT I SAY
> WAKE ME AT 7.30 AND MAKE ME GET UP
> ———
> TRY AGAIN AT 10.30

He was perhaps better trained for future emergencies than a man who really meant to get up early, and did not.

But there are others, who, when the early hour comes, and the body pleads for more sleep, sit up in bed and before rising, thus address the body: "You don't want to get

THE COURAGE

up at 7.30? Very well, tomorrow you will rise at 6.30. And then, if I hear one squawk from you, the next day you will rise at 5.30. We shall find out, you and I, who is master here." A well-disciplined mind in control of a well-disciplined body, will go far.

The individual against the crowd, the plainly named individual against the powerful anonymous compact majority, is an inspiring spectacle for those who come after, even if we are not able ourselves to rise to such heights. In 1794, during a trial in Scotland for sedition, the one unpardonable sin against the religion of nationalism, the prisoner named Skirving, alone and friendless in a court room filled with a crowd thirsty for his blood, was sharply addressed by Justice Braxfield, sitting in the panoply of power. Skirving turned and

OF IGNORANCE

said, "It is altogether unavailing for your Lordship to menace me, for I have long learned to fear not the face of man."

Well, they hanged Skirving; they broke his neck, but they could not break his heart.

Many other historic instances might be given; but I like to think of the vast number of humble individuals, who will never be mentioned in the history books, and yet who have exhibited in crushing disasters and also in the daily struggle of life, the most splendid courage. I know many women, whose husbands have died or who have never had any, who are quite alone, not only without influential friends but without any daily companions, and with almost no financial resources, who face every day with calm cheerfulness, making no complaints and asking no favours.

THE COURAGE

While years of depression destroy many persons, they have also the one and only redeeming feature of war. They bring out heroism in unsuspected places. In the present year of grace, America is full of heroic men and women, who are meeting terrible hardships with steadily increasing fortitude. Human nature is being tested.

And the vast number of High School and College graduates, who are going out into a world that apparently does not want them, are showing a spirit that increases and strengthens our faith in youth. Courage has always been needed and seldom more than now.

I will mention two instances of courage that have come within my own personal knowledge.

A woman of noble character (now with God), happily married, became a widow

OF IGNORANCE

while still young, and was left with two baby boys. She brought them up carefully, and they entered the same class in a great university. One was graduated valedictorian, the other fourth in his class. Shortly after graduation, one of them died of typhoid fever. The other had a nervous breakdown, and went away to a sanatorium. A newspaper reporter woke the lonely woman at two o'clock in the morning, and informed her that her son had committed suicide by cutting his throat. Some time after this, she lost nearly her whole fortune within twenty-four hours. A year or two after that, she was stricken without any warning by total blindness and never saw the light again. I used to call upon her and talk about things in general. I never heard her utter one word of complaint, I never heard her mention her own tragedies as if they were unusual. We talked about the news of the day, politics and general literature, poetry, music and art. She was a devout Christian, but she never talked sanctimoniously. I never heard her quote Scripture; I never heard her say, "The Lord has given and the Lord has taken away." She faced the daily darkness with a calm and quiet mind.

And I know another lady still living, though well past eighty, whose husband died some years ago, both of whose sons, men of really remarkable ability and usefulness, died, whose only daughter, an admirable professional teacher, died of a long and painful illness, and who herself has been for years totally blind. Far from complaining, she is cheerful and interested in life; she says that in her blindness, instead

OF IGNORANCE

of living in blackness, she feels she is living in light.

I give these two instances for the strengthening of hearts.

It takes far more courage to live well than to die well. I do not particularly admire the criminals who face the gallows and the chair with a jest. We read how the man was led to the chair; he laughed at the chaplain, and inhaling a cigarette, said to the electrician, "Step on it!" This is often spoken of as if it were fortitude. But this criminal faced a death far easier than the kind of death most of us must endure; and with a group of people around him, he found it not very difficult to die without flinching. What he could not do was to live courageously.

I often mildly wonder that so few politi-

THE COURAGE

cians are courageous. Why don't they realise that sometimes courage is a political asset? As a matter of fact, while great intelligence is rare in politicians, it is not so rare as courage. And yet there are statesmen who have won an enduring fame mainly by courage. The latest biography of Grover Cleveland, the admirable book by Allan Nevins, which was justly awarded the Pulitzer Prize, lays its main emphasis on courage. The full title of the book is *Grover Cleveland: A Study in Courage.* Grover Cleveland rose from Sheriff of Buffalo to President of the United States on a continual series of vetoes. His one dominating quality was Courage, and as a result he ranks among our most admired presidents.

In the long run, the people like a man who is not afraid of them. When Campbell-

OF IGNORANCE

Bannerman, speaking in the House of Commons during the Boer War, described the British as using "methods of barbarism," it was believed not only by his enemies but by his friends, that his career was closed. In a very few years he was Prime Minister.

When John Stuart Mill consented to run for Parliament, he made so many conditions that one of the committee who called on him said, "God Almighty could not be elected on that platform!" Possibly not; but they elected Mill. In the course of the campaign, at a public meeting where he was to address an audience composed mainly of laborers, an enemy had printed an enormous placard on which appeared the statement signed by Mill, to the effect that the working-classes were generally liars. He was asked if he had really said that and he un-

THE COURAGE

hesitatingly replied in the affirmative. Immediately a tremendous cheering came from the crowd of workingmen, who were glad and surprised to see and hear an honest and fearless man.

During his service as Representative in Congress from Michigan, the Honourable Louis C. Cramton was asked to explain in public why he had voted against the expressed wishes of his constituents. He replied that he had been elected not as a rubber stamp, but as an independent man who would use his knowledge for what he conceived to be the best interests of the country as a whole. He was re-elected by an increased majority.

Superb illustrations of the courage of ignorance are found in the lives of three explorers of the Antarctic—Amundsen, Shackleton, and Scott. Amundsen was the

OF IGNORANCE

first man to reach the South Pole; then, with Lincoln Ellsworth, he flew across the North Pole. Finally, he gave his life in a voluntary search for another missing explorer.

When Shackleton and his men were lost in the Antarctic ice, he told them they must try to go on foot many miles in order to reach safety. That it would be necessary to throw away every superfluous burden. The men threw away extra clothing, extra food, and many other necessities. Shackleton took a handful of gold sovereigns and dropped them through a crevice in the ice to the bottom of the southern ocean. Then he took from his pocket a copy of the poems of Robert Browning, and told his men that he would not throw away this book, because it would give them more strength than food or clothing or shelter.

THE COURAGE

In January 1912 Captain Robert Scott realised the ambition of his life—he and his men reached the South Pole. But only to find that Amundsen had reached it a few weeks before; they cheered for Amundsen and started north. During the month of March, they were caught in a blizzard and all died. One member of the expedition, Captain Oates, walked out alone and perished in the ice, hoping thereby to save his comrades. When it became evident that no one could survive, Scott wrote some letters to friends at home, not knowing whether they would ever reach them, but taking the chance. Here is one to Sir James Barrie:

> We are pegging out in a very comfortless spot. Hoping this letter may be found and sent to you, I write a word of farewell. . . . I think this makes an

OF IGNORANCE

example for Englishmen of the future. . . . Good-bye. I am not at all afraid of the end, but sad to miss many a humble pleasure which I had planned for the future on our long marches. I may not have proved a great explorer, but we have done the greatest march ever made. . . . We are in a desperate state, feet frozen: &c. No fuel and a long way from food, but it would do your heart good to be in our tent, to hear our songs and the cheery conversation as to what we will do when we get to Hut Point.

Later. We are very near the end, but have not and will not lose our good cheer. We have had four days of storm in our tent and nowhere's food or fuel. We did intend to finish ourselves when things proved like this, but we have decided to die naturally in the track. . . . I never met a man in my life whom I admired and loved more than you, but I never could show you how much your friendship meant to me, for you had much to give and I nothing.

This is the perfect example of the cour-

THE COURAGE

age of ignorance. Scott did not know that these letters would ever be found. The chances were against it. How much easier it was to commit suicide and avoid the last slow agonies! What must the final survivor have thought as he looked around at the frozen corpses of his comrades? But they took the hardest way. They decided to "die naturally," why? Because they were English gentlemen, brought up in a great tradition of manhood. They wished to be worthy of their breeding and their ideals. They could not *know* that this sacrifice would make any difference.

But the bodies were found, the letters were found, and we know that for the next thousand years the serene courage of Captain Scott and his men will inspire millions of human beings.

OF IGNORANCE

Every act of individual courage elevates the human race.

On Scott's tomb they placed the last line of Tennyson's poem "Ulysses."

> *To strive, to seek, to find, and not to yield.*

There can be no true courage, there can be no true virtue, without ignorance. If there is the certainty of profit or reward, the courage and the virtue lose their integrity. It is often said that honesty is the best policy. But if any one behaves honestly because he thinks it is the best policy, then he is not really honest. As a matter of fact, absolute honesty is not always the best policy. If one is looking merely for success, it would be wiser to be honest most of the

THE COURAGE

time, at least until one had gained a convenient reputation for honesty. Then it would be wise to cheat at the psychological moment.

A man must have an ideal outside of himself to be either honest or brave. He must show courage not because he thinks it will pay, but because he believes courage is a good quality of character. When the barkeeper told Peter Stirling, "Dat aint de way," Peter replied, "It will be my way."

In the last poem of the English poet laureate, Robert Bridges, written when he was past eighty years of age, he tells admiringly of an incident in the life of the Spartan general Brasidas, who lived in the Fifth Century before Christ and who died in battle. Although he was a Spartan, he was a diplomat, a man of great personal charm, with gracious manners and a sense of humour. One day a captured mouse bit him. Brasidas was about to crush it, when suddenly he thought of the tremendous courage of a mouse biting a Spartan general; he burst out laughing and let the mouse go, because the man of war admired courage. We hear the laugh of that soldier across all the centuries!

Bridges in his poem says he is glad the Spartan did not kill the mouse; and so am I, because it showed a certain humorous and sympathetic consideration, the one who was bitten actually appreciating the merit of the biter. This is unusual.

But not to make a mountain out of a mouse, I do not regard the attack of the mouse as a display of courage. It is really an illustration of what I spoke of early in this book, it is an illustration not of true courage. It illustrates something quite different—the courage of Despair. If a rat is cornered by a terrier, the rat does not acquiesce in his own dissolution, as much as to say, "Please come and eat me." No, the rat fights; but it fights blindly, with the courage of despair; the only courage left in many modern philosophers.

Humanity has a right to the courage, not of despair, and not of knowledge; it has a right to the courage of Hope. When Captain Scott decided to die "naturally," he was ignorant as to the result of such a decision. But it was the courage of hope. And I do not mean the hope that the letters would be found, though he had that hope. I mean the hope that the core of the universe is eternally *right*. That honesty and courage and self-sacrifice are really better than cheating and cowardice and greed.

In his essay "Pulvis et Umbra," Steven-

OF IGNORANCE

son, after saying everything that could be said against the rewards of integrity, finally came to this conclusion:

> And as we dwell, we living things, in our isle of terror and under the imminent hand of death, God forbid it should be man the erected, the reasoner, the wise in his own eyes—God forbid it should be man that wearies in welldoing, that despairs of unrewarded effort, or utters the language of complaint. Let it be enough for faith, that the whole creation groans in mortal frailty, strives with unconquerable constancy: surely not all in vain.

There is the false courage of ignorance, which arises either from foolhardiness or stupidity. He didn't know the drawbridge was open; he didn't know it was loaded.

But the true courage of ignorance is the courage that faces the unknown outcome

COURAGE OF IGNORANCE

with serenity. As has been well said, a calm mind is a victorious mind. And even if the result should be defeat in the practical undertaking, there remains always one victory —the victory over oneself.

THE END